B.B. WOLF
SAUSAGE
HAMHOCKS
BACON
PORK CHOPS

Ed's parts

C.C.R.W #6

## For Barbara, the fourth artist

### EDITOR'S NOTE

Three is a special and often powerful number. So when three members of the same talented family come to you with a three-part project that they all want to work on together, you had better pay attention. Ed, Rebecca, and Michael each bring something uniquely interesting and fresh to the creative party, and my relationship with each of them is different. The mix of admiration, exasperation, and affection that often results from the editor–author–illustrator relationship is usually present whenever I work on a book with any one of them. Need I say it tripled in this case? The result of their work, however, pleases me greatly. We are triply enriched to have this sketchbook of occasional pieces — many of which have something to do with the concept of three — to savor and go back to repeatedly. Thank you thrice, Emberleys, for this energetic work. It does indeed show the power of three.

—J.K.

First Edition

Library of Congress Cataloging-in-Publication Data

Emberley, Ed.
    Three : an Emberley family sketchbook / by Ed, Rebecca, and Michael Emberley.
        p.    cm.
    Summary: Ed Emberley and his children, Rebecca and Michael, present a collection of original works, most of which use the number or concept of three.
    ISBN 0-316-23506-7
    1. Three (The number) — Literary collections.    [1. Three (The number) — Literary collections.]    I. Emberley, Rebecca.    II. Emberley, Michael.    III. Title.
    PZ5.E485Th  1998
    [Fic] — dc21                                                                                        97-39286

10 9 8 7 6 5 4 3 2 1

TWP

Published simultaneously in Canada by Little, Brown & Company (Canada) Limited

Printed in Singapore

# THREE

## AN EMBERLEY FAMILY SKETCHBOOK

# BY ED, REBECCA, & MICHAEL EMBERLEY

Little, Brown and Company
BOSTON NEW YORK TORONTO LONDON

Hello, my name is Ed Emberley.
This is my wife, Barbara.

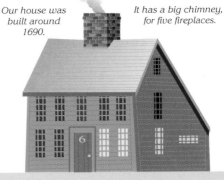

*Our house was built around 1690.*

*It has a big chimney, for five fireplaces.*

We live in an old red house
in a small town
forty-five minutes north
of Boston, Massachusetts.

We do not have pets, but
woodchucks, mice, ants, toads,
swans, and other creatures
visit us from time to time.

SNIP
SNAP
SNIP

I am the father of
Rebecca Emberley

SCRITCH
SCRATCH
SCRITCH

and Michael Emberley.

BEEP
BOOP
BEEP

I made my pictures for this book
using my computer.

For my hobbies I like:
paddling my kayak when it's
warm and sunny,

cross-country skiing
when it's cold and snowy,

and reading in a cozy chair
when it's dark and rainy.

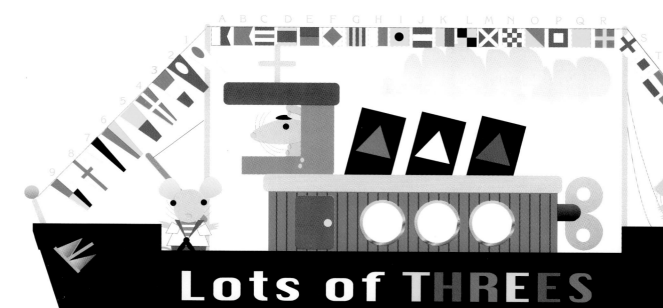

# Lots of THREES

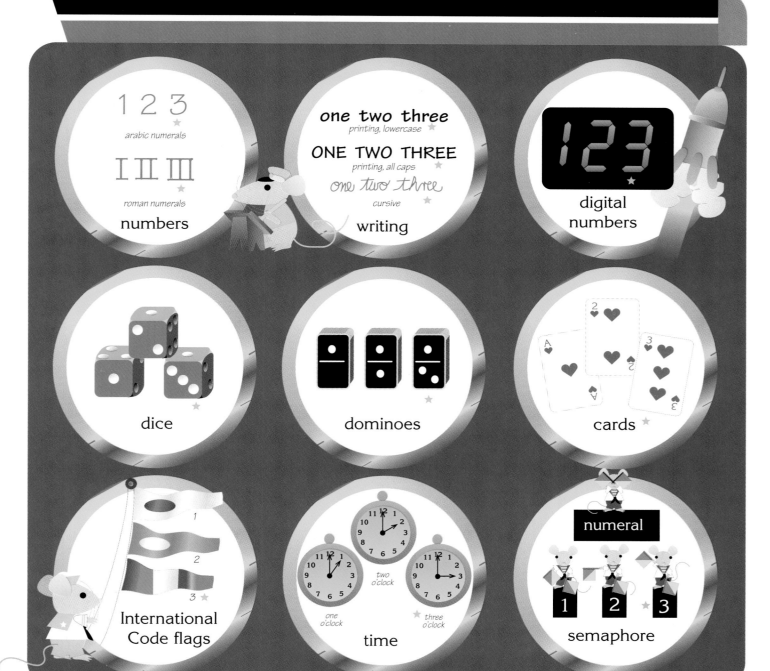

1 2 3
*arabic numerals* ★

I II III
*roman numerals* ★

**numbers**

**one two three**
printing, lowercase ★

**ONE TWO THREE**
printing, all caps ★

*one two three*
cursive ★

**writing**

123
★

**digital numbers**

**dice** ★

**dominoes** ★

**cards** ★

1
2
3 ★

**International Code flags**

two o'clock

one o'clock ★ three o'clock

**time**

numeral

1 2 3 ★

**semaphore**

# Other Ways to Say
# One, Two, Three

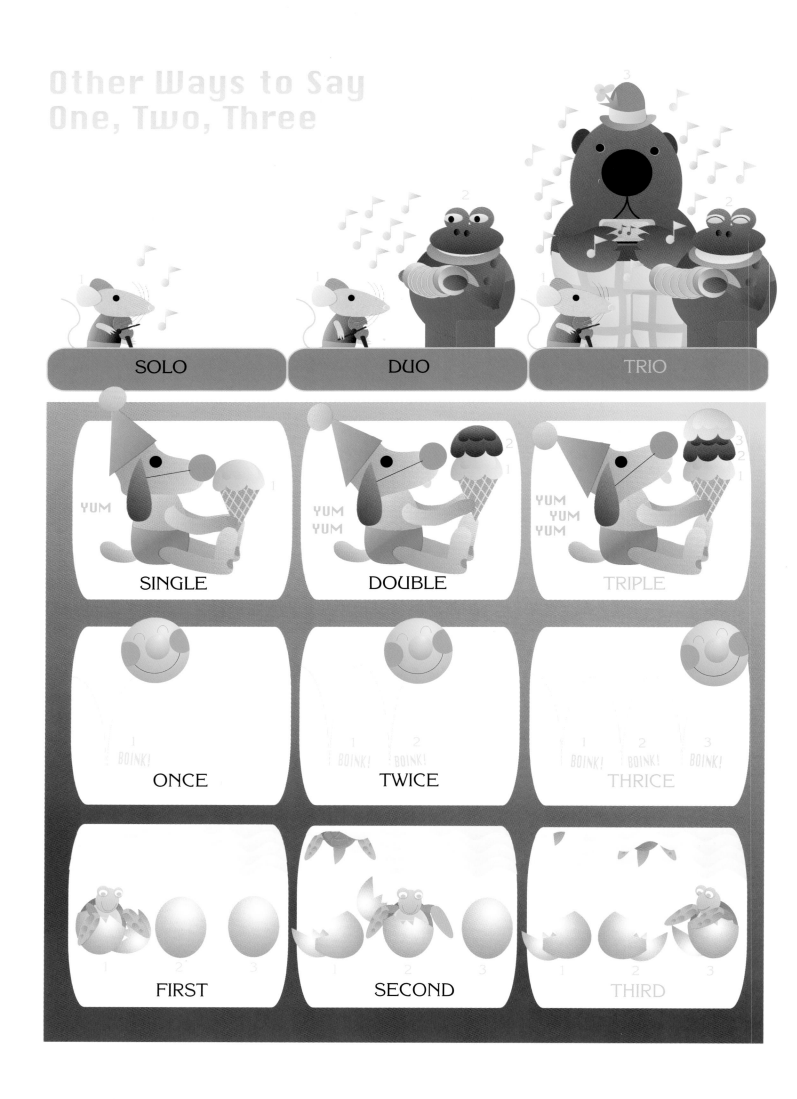

SOLO

DUO

TRIO

SINGLE

DOUBLE

TRIPLE

ONCE

TWICE

THRICE

FIRST

SECOND

THIRD

# Some Three Things

**TRICERATOPS**
*dinosaur with three horns*

**TRIANGLE**
*shape with three sides*

**TRIPOD**
*camera stand with three legs*

**TRIDENT**
*spear with three points*

**TRICYCLE**
*cycle with three wheels*

**TRIMARAN**
*boat with three hulls*

**TRIPLANE**
*airplane with three wings*

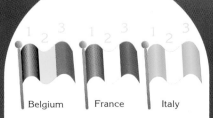

Belgium    France    Italy

**TRICOLOR**
*flag with three stripes*

**TRICORN**
*hat with three corners*

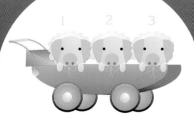

**TRIPLETS**
*three babies with the same
birthday and the same parents*

# ★BING ★ BANG★ BOOM★

Or why Charlie Green, Sally Blue, and Brown Bear were late for Violet Violet's birthday party

Ed Emberley's Make Believe Snap Together Blocks

Snap

VROOM
VROOM
VROOM

Beep
Beep

VROOM

Beep
Beep

UP

VROOM

Beep
Beep

DOWN

Beep          Beep

VROOM

IN

OUT

VROOM

# How to Draw Three "3" Things

Some things are hard to draw; some things are easy.
Here are three easy things.
Just start by drawing a 3, then add a few simple lines.

First draw your 3.
Then turn it till it
looks like this ...
and this.

3 extras for
experts

# How to Make a "Cut-and-Paste" Triangle Cat

Ed made this triangle cat using his computer. You can use a computer, or you can use scissors, paste, and a marker.

**1**

Make 5 squares:
2 black 8"
1 green 4"
1 pink 2"
1 red 1"

**2**

Make triangles from your squares:
1. Fold and crease.
2. Unfold.
3. Cut.

**3**

You'll make your cat
from these 7 triangles:
2 black 8"
1 green 4"
1 pink 2"
1 red 1"

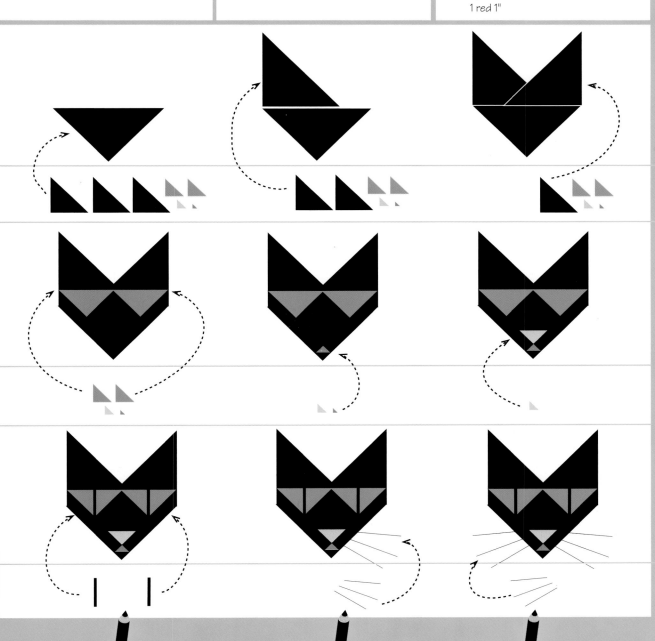

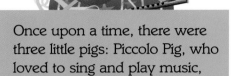 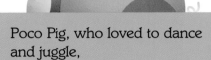

Once upon a time, A Fairy Tale Trilogy there were three ...

Once upon a time, there were three little pigs: Piccolo Pig, who loved to sing and play music,

Poco Pig, who loved to dance and juggle,

and Practical Pig, who loved to make things.

Once upon a time, there were three bears: Papa Bear,

Mama Bear,

and Baby Bear.

Once upon a time, there were three Billy Goats Gruff: Little Billy Goat Gruff,

Middle Billy Goat Gruff,

and Big Billy Goat Gruff.

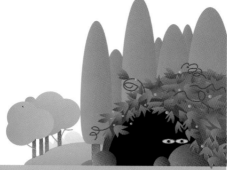

They lived at one end of a pretty green valley.

At the other end of the valley was a deep, dark cave.

In the cave lived a big, bad wolf, whose favorite food was pig.

They lived in a little cabin in the middle of a deep, dark wood.

At the edge of the wood was a little yellow cottage.

In the cottage lived a little girl named Goldilocks, whose favorite food was porridge.

They lived on the bank of a river.

Over the river was a bridge.

Under the bridge lived a mean, old troll, whose favorite food was goat.

Piccolo Pig built a house of straw.

Poco Pig built a house of sticks.

Practical Pig built a house of bricks.

One morning Mama Bear made some porridge and put it into three bowls.

Baby Bear put them on the table to cool.

Papa Bear had an idea.

They were running out of grass on their side of the river,

but they could see lots of sweet, green grass on the other side of the river.

However, the river was too wide to jump, too deep to wade, and too swift to swim.

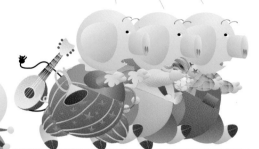

So the days went by, with Poco dancing, Piccolo playing, and Practical building.

At the end of summer, there was bad news.

The three pigs ran to their homes.

So the three bears went out to pick some berries.

Goldilocks saw the bears leaving.

She decided to go into their cottage and look around.

And unfortunately, the mean, old troll ate any goat who tried to cross the bridge.

The troll was big, the troll was strong, but luckily, the troll was also incredibly stupid.

So the three Billy Goats made a plan.

First the wolf went to Piccolo Pig's straw house and banged on the door.

He tried to get Piccolo Pig to open the door.

But Piccolo Pig would not open the door.

Goldilocks tasted Papa Bear's porridge, but it was too hot.

She tasted Mama Bear's porridge, but it was too cold.

She tasted Baby Bear's porridge, and it was just right, so she ate it all up.

Little Billy Goat Gruff started across the bridge.

The mean, old troll heard his hoofbeats

and came up on the bridge.

HUFF, HUFF, HUFF!

PUFF, PUFF, PUFF!

So the wolf took a big breath

and blew the straw to pieces. While the wolf was catching his breath,

Piccolo Pig ran away to Poco Pig's house.

HMM!

HRUMPH!

WHEE!

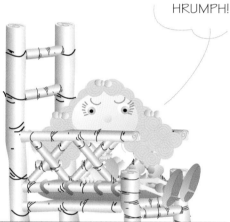

Goldilocks sat in Papa Bear's chair, but it was too high.

She sat in Mama Bear's chair, but it was too low.

She sat in Baby Bear's chair, and it was just right, so she rocked until she broke it all up.

OH, PLEASE, MR. TROLL, DON'T EAT ME. I'LL JUST MAKE A SNACK. WAIT FOR MY BROTHER MIDDLE BILLY GOAT GRUFF. HE WILL MAKE A WHOLE MEAL.

HMM, SNACK OR MEAL? SNACK OR MEAL?

Then Little Billy Goat Gruff told his story.

The troll thought about it

and let Little Billy Goat Gruff go over to the sweet, green grass.

CIMARRON ELEMENTARY SCHOOL

Next, the wolf went to Poco Pig's stick house and banged on the door.

He tried to get Poco Pig to open the door.

But Poco Pig would not open the door.

Goldilocks tried Papa Bear's bed, but it was too hard.

She tried Mama Bear's bed, but it was too soft.

She tried Baby Bear's bed, and it was just right, so she got in and fell fast asleep.

Next, Middle Billy Goat Gruff started across the bridge.

The mean, old troll heard his hoofbeats

and came up on the bridge.

HUFF, HUFF, HUFF!

PUFF, PUFF, PUFF!

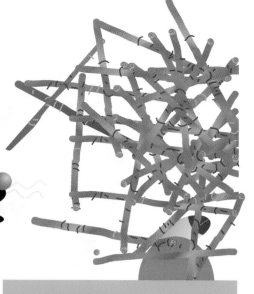

So the wolf took a big breath

and blew the stick house to pieces. While the wolf was catching his breath,

Piccolo Pig and Poco Pig ran away to Practical Pig's house.

SOMEBODY'S BEEN EATING MY PORRIDGE!

SOMEBODY'S BEEN EATING **MY** PORRIDGE!

SOMEBODY'S BEEN EATING **MY** PORRIDGE! AND ATE IT ALL UP!

When the three bears came home, Papa Bear looked at his porridge bowl.

Mama Bear looked at her porridge bowl.

Then Baby Bear looked at his porridge bowl.

OH, PLEASE, MR. TROLL, DON'T EAT ME. I'LL JUST MAKE A MEAL. WAIT FOR MY BROTHER BIG BILLY GOAT GRUFF. HE WILL MAKE A FEAST.

HMMM, MEAL OR FEAST? MEAL OR FEAST?

Then Middle Billy Goat Gruff told his story.

The troll thought about it

and let Middle Billy Goat Gruff go over to the sweet, green grass.

Then the wolf went to Practical Pig's brick house and banged on the door.

He tried to get Practical Pig to open the door.

But Practical Pig would not open the door.

Next, Papa Bear looked at his chair.

Mama Bear looked at her chair.

Then Baby Bear looked at his chair.

Finally, Big Billy Goat Gruff started across the bridge.

The mean, old troll heard his hoofbeats

and came up on the bridge.

So the wolf took a big breath

and blew, and blew, and blew,

but he could not blow the brick house to pieces.

Papa Bear looked at his bed.

Mama Bear looked at her bed.

Then Baby Bear looked at his bed.

Then Big Billy Goat Gruff told his story. [Of course there was no **Great Big** Billy Goat Gruff.

Big Billy Goat Gruff was just trying to fool the mean, old troll.] The troll thought about it

but would not let Big Billy Goat Gruff go over the bridge to the sweet, green grass.

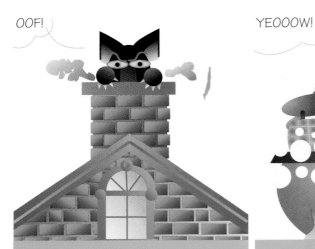

So he scrambled up onto the roof and slid down the chimney

into a pot of boiling water that Practical Pig had put on the fire.

The wolf jumped back up the chimney, slid back down the roof,

Goldilocks woke up, saw the three bears, hopped out of bed,

and ran all the way home. When the the three bears saw that she was just a little girl,

they had a good laugh. Then Mama Bear made some fresh porridge.

They butted the mean, old troll, and he flew up in the air,

fell into the deep, wide, swift-flowing river,

and was never heard from again.

OWOOOOO!

and jumped into the river to cool off.

GLUG! GLUG! GLUG!

He floated away and was never seen again. After that, Piccolo made music, Poco

danced and juggled, Practical took care of the rest, and they all lived happily ever after.

HEE, HEE, HEE!

Baby Bear sprinkled some berries on top.

HO, HO, HO!

And Papa Bear fixed Baby Bear's rocking chair.

Goldilocks went home and had a nice hot supper, and they all lived happily ever after.

Not only was there lots of sweet, green grass on the other side of the river.

There was also Lilly, Tilly, and Milly Goat Gruff.

And they all lived happily ever after.

# REBECCA

FAMILY PHOTO, 1993

KINDERGARTEN ART

Hi, my name is Rebecca Emberley. Welcome to my section of the Emberley family sketchbook. This project is unlike any other I have worked on. Being able to illustrate whatever I want rather than having it all fit one story or concept is very unusual and wonderful. I found out all kinds of new things. I tried several different mediums, from woodcuts to appliqué. I also found out that I really like to write poetry. I had not written poetry in many, many years. It was hard to choose the eight poems that I used in the book! I had a lot of fun experimenting in this book. I hope you enjoy looking at my work as much as I enjoyed doing it.

A FEW YEARS LATER, 1960s

HIGH-SCHOOL ART—YIKES!

SOME EARLY CUT PAPER, 1970s

1960
I AM TWO; MICHAEL IS
ABOUT SIX MONTHS.

LOOKS ABOUT 1967, ON THE BOAT
AM I DRAWING?

I AM GUESSING 1974
HIGH-SCHOOL TRACK TEAM

I live and work in Newburyport, Massachusetts. I live there with my daughter, Adrian, my husband, Bill, and our three cats, Tao, Smokey, and Nightingale. Adrian is twelve right now, and she is a big help. The cats are not.

I have a studio in my house. It is very small and very messy. Most of the artwork that I do is from cut paper, and there is paper every-where. And I mean EVERYWHERE—on the floor, on the walls, piled up on the table and shelves. There is also paint and glitter, ribbons and beads, pens, pencils—all manner of thing. Even when I'm not working, I like to make things.

I also like to hike and ski. I sew and I read a lot. I like to travel, but I also love living in New England. I have lived in many places, including Colorado and Florida, but I really love the change of seasons.

I get my ideas from many different places. The more I look, listen, and read, the more ideas I get.

ADRIAN IS BORN, 1985
WOW, IS SHE SMALL!

ADRIAN AND I, 1997

ADRIAN, 1997

I ran into the forest one dark night
and gave myself a terrible fright.

The trees were blowing in the breeze,
moaning, groaning, shedding leaves.

Eyes were blinking, winking, thinking,
I CAN SEE YOU, BUT YOU CAN'T SEE ME,
BECAUSE I'M HIDING IN A TREE.

Things were rustling, bustling, scratching,
while in my head ideas were hatching.

Is it tigers
or is it mice?
Is it monsters
who'll bite me thrice?

And when I thought my heart would burst,
I turned and yelled, "Come catch me first!"

I ran out of the forest one dark night
'cause I gave myself a terrible fright.

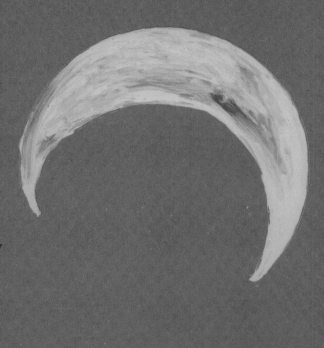

Three peas in a pod—
it's really not odd.
We've lived in here
all of our life.

We wait for the day
when we get out and play
on a plate
with a fork and a knife.

They chase and we run—
believe me, it's fun.
But as soon as they catch us,
we're done.

So for now it's just fine
to hang on the vine,
1-2-3 peas in a pod.

When I grow up
I want to be
not 1, not 2,
but part of 3.

# Rupert and Alison

Rupert and Alison loved to cook.
They kept their recipes in a great big book.
Some were good, and some were not;
some were only gobbledygook.

Rupert and Alison didn't worry.
They loved to cook in a great big flurry.
When things did not turn out quite right,
Rupert and Alison added more curry.

If you look inside their book,
you'll see the clever route they took.
They wrote their recipes down in threes
so they could remember them all with ease.

Here are some of the best of these:

# Gobbledygook

3 tbsp. butter
3 cups marshmallows
3/4 cup peanut butter
3 cups crispy rice cereal
3 tbsp. sesame seeds
1/3 cup chopped dried apricots
1/3 cup chocolate chips

Melt butter in a large pot or pan over low heat.
Add marshmallows, and stir until melted. Add
peanut butter; mix well. Remove from heat. Add
cereal and sesame seeds; mix well. This will now be
really gunky and gooky. After it has cooled a
litle, add the apricots and chocolate chips.

Now, if you don't like to get messy, scoop all
this out into an 8" x 8" pan (like a brownie pan)
and let it cool completely. Then cut it into
squares. But if you like to get messy, scoop out
the gobbledygook with a spoon, roll it into balls,
and set them to cool on a cookie sheet. Then lick
your fingers. Rupert and Alison would approve.

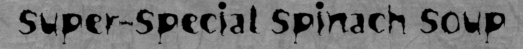

# super-special spinach soup

3 cans chicken broth

1/3 cup rice

3 big squeezes lemon juice

3 big handfuls fresh spinach,
  rinsed and rinsed and rinsed

3 quick turns black pepper per bowlful

Bring the broth to a boil in a saucepan. Add rice.
Turn heat down to simmer. When rice is soft, turn
off heat. Add your big squeezes of lemon juice.
(Look out for seeds!) Get out your soup bowls.
Shred the spinach leaves, and divide them between
your bowls. Pour the hot broth and rice over the
spinach leaves. Add pepper. VOILÀ! Super-Special
Spinach Soup!

# Never-Worry Chicken Curry

3 single chicken breasts
3 tbsp. butter or oil
2/3 cup chopped onion
3 tbsp. curry powder
2/3 cup evaporated skim milk

Cut chicken into bite-size pieces. Heat butter or oil in a large sauté pan over medium heat. Add the onion, and stir until it gets a little soft. Add curry powder, and stir a few more times. Now add chicken and sauté (this means stir some more). The curry will start to gunk up and seem a little dry. This is OK. Just don't let it burn. When the chicken is not slimy and pink anymore, it should be firm and white (well, it will be yellow from the curry). Add the evaporated skim milk. Now it will be soupy. Lower the heat a little and just keep stirring, and it will start to thicken up. Keep stirring! When it is as thick as you like it, it's done.

A note from Rupert and Alison: Stirring is key to this recipe, as you can see. Sometimes practice stirring is necessary. If food is flying all over the stove, you are stirring too fast! If the food is burning, you are stirring too slow! We know, we know, this sounds hard, but it's not.

And remember, never worry—you can always add more curry.

Three slippery, slimy snakes went on a thrilling ride: down the hole in front

Two slippery, slimy snakes went on a thrilling ride: down the hole

One slippery, slimy snake

Two went in, and one came out.
And though she shouted all about,
there was only one slip-slimy snake.

down the hole

of them and out the other side.

Three went in, and two came out. And though they shouted all about, there were only two slip-slimy snakes.

in front of them and out the other side.

went on a thrilling ride:

in front of her and out the other side.

One went in, and one came out, and so she shouted all about, "I am the very best slip-slimy snake!"

It's raining today,
so I can't go and play.
The clouds are growling;
the wind is howling.
Rain is splashing, smashing the flowers.
Lightning is crashing for what seems like hours.

Hey, my friend Stella
just blew by with her umbrella!

I couldn't;
I shouldn't.
I'll just take a peek.
Oh, no, my clothing is starting to leak!
The rain has got in from my neck to my feet.
Yet I run down the sidewalk, hoping to meet

my friend Stella
with her umbrella.

But I'm stopped in my tracks
by a huge bolt of lightning,
which I will admit
is extremely frightening!

Forget about Stella—
I'll just have to tell her,

I couldn't,
I shouldn't,
go out to play
because it is definitely raining today.

I once knew a great green crocodile.
You very rarely saw him smile.
For on his head he had three spots
and on these spots he had three dots.
The other crocodiles, they had four.
He desperately wanted one spot more.
"Why do I have only three?
There must be something wrong with me."

He cried and cried, great green tears.
He went on like this, it seemed, for years.
One day a bird flew from the brush
and told the crocodile to hush!
"Did you ever think that what you've got
is special simply for what it's not?"

The crocodile gave a startled roar.
He thought of something he hadn't before.
Maybe, he thought, less is more.
He gave a great green toothy grin
and lifted up his great green chin.
"Bird," he said, "you may be right!"
Then he hugged that bird with all his might!

We danced around the fire
for three long frenzied nights.
The wolves they howled,
the cats they hissed,
the field mice got in fights.

The drummers drummed
a primal beat,
we kicked and clawed
and stomped our feet.
We whirled and twirled
around and round
and thrashed our tails
upon the ground.

We yipped and yowled,
the bears they growled,
our voices carrying higher.
The lizards scratched,
while turtles hatched
by the heat that
came from the fire.

Then, with the third and final dawn,
we gave a great collective yawn.
We smoothed our feathers, fur, and fins,
and so another year begins.

# MICHAEL EMBERLEY

## Who is Michael Emberley?

I am a tall, skinny guy who wears glasses, rides a bicycle a lot, and works in an old factory in the city of Boston. I look something like this ➡

I get paid money to draw pictures and write stories for kids. I do not get paid to ride a bike.

When I'm not wearing a helmet, I look like this ➡

or this ➡      or this ➡

I almost never wear a helmet when I draw, but I always wear one when I ride my bike.

This is my studio. It always looks this messy.

All my drawing supplies are on one side, my napping couches and books are on the other, and my six bicycles are all over the place. I have a microwave and a mini-refrigerator to make snacks and keep drinks cold.

I am the son of **Ed Emberley** and the brother of **Rebecca Emberley,** the other two artists in this book. My father likes to use computers for his art. My sister likes to use paper and scissors.

I like to use pencils, pens, watercolors, and pastels.

**This is my father.** He is a sailor, skier, artist, and designer. He wears a helmet, but only in his kayak.

**My mother** looks like this. She is an artist, craftsperson, chef, and accountant. She wears a helmet, but only on her mountain bike .

**This is my sister.** She is an artist, writer, and designer. She never wears a helmet.

I carry sketchbooks around with me when I travel, and I draw the people and places I see.

I do not have any pets because most animals make me sneeze.

I own six bicycles but have never owned a car.

Sometimes I come back from a bike ride and just start working dressed like this. When I'm drawing, I sit at my drawing table. When I'm writing, I lie down on my couch. If I decide to take a nap, I take off my helmet.

# The Reptile Rumba

The new reptile rumba,
  our favorite numba',
    is every hip dinosaur's pick.
  We wiggle and rumble,
    you'll see no one stumble,
with a one, two, three,
  step, turn, and kick.
  In big groups or pairs,
    all alone, no one cares,
      no other new step does the trick.
        All beasts move together;
          we're light as a feather
            as we twist and we twirl
            and we sway.
            This dinosaur dance
              has us lost in a trance;
                rumba rhythm just sweeps us away.
          Take a turn if you dare,
      fling your tail in the air,
be a reptile and rumba today!

# Waves

The ocean with a thunderous roar
crashes waves up on the shore.
They swell and surge like green sea mountains,
spitting spray like giant fountains.
One wave, two waves, three waves, four,
they never end—there's always more.
They foam and finish on the sand,
but no one knows where they began.

# Three Honey Bunnies

See three honey-colored bunnies,
with some money from their mummy,
go to find the yellow parrot's carrot truck.

See three honey-colored bunnies,
with three hungry rumbly tummies,
find the yellow parrot's carrot truck, stuck up.

See three honey-colored bunnies
find the trouble in a hurry.
Soon that yellow parrot's carrot truck's
fixed up.

To reward those honey bunnies,
yellow parrot takes no money.
Then he gives those honey bunnies,
with three hungry rumbly tummies,
three enormous yellow carrot treats for free.

# Row, Row, Row Your Boat

Row, row, row your boat
gently down the stream.
Merrily, merrily, merrily, merrily,
life is but a dream.

# Three Baby Monkeys

Three baby monkeys jumping on the bed.
One fell off and bumped his head.

The mama came in, and the mama monkey said,
"No baby monkeys jumping on the bed!"

Two baby monkeys jumping on the bed.
One fell off and bumped his head.

The papa came in, and the papa monkey said,
"No baby monkeys jumping on the bed!"

One baby monkey jumping on the bed.
The baby monkey jumps and bumps his head.

The doctor came in, and the doctor said,
"Baby wants to be with his brothers instead!"

# The Music Makers

The music's inside, and then it escapes.
It's liquid and lazy, and then it takes shape.
It buzzes the air; it rumbles the ground,
flying notes chasing each other around.
Drum bangers, brass blowers,
sliding trombones,
strummers and shakers and
gold saxophones.

The players are teasing and tickling time —
this way and that way,
it falls, then it climbs.
Playing in trios, duets, or alone,
jangling rhythms and
tangling tones,

the fresh music makers
are mixing up sounds.
They're spinning our hearing,
they're drowning our frowns.

# This Jane's a Pain

Though Jane is just an average name,
this Jane is not your average Jane.
I really could at length explain,
but, in short, this Jane's a pain.

I should be nice and not complain;
poor little thing, it's such a shame,
so pink, so young, yet all the same,
I wish she'd just slip down the drain.

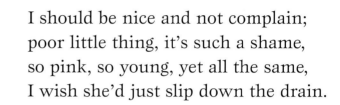

Would someone buy this pain called Jane?
She doesn't scratch, she's completely tame,
she's never been left out in the rain.
No fuss, no mess, we've got her trained.

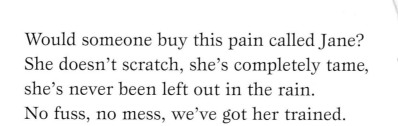

"Please, sir, I would like to complain.
This Jane is really much too strange.
She has no hair; she might have mange.
Look! She crawls—I think she's lame.

"Is there some deal we could arrange?
Any more Janes in our price range?
Can we return her in exchange
For some nice Jane who's not a pain?"

Perhaps I'll take Jane on a plane,
then on some tiny local train;

I'll leave her in the baggage claim,
then quietly come home again.

It's not her fault,
she's not to blame.
She has such a tiny brain.
I guess we'll keep her—

All the same, I can't forget,
this Jane's a pain!

# Three Chances

I found a baby bumble bee.
I'm gonna take him home with me.
He's soft and cute as cute can be.
He'll play with me upon my

OUCH!

I caught a naughty bumble bee.
I may not take him home with me.
You must be careful with a bee
'cause if you don't, he'll try to

OUCH!

I've got a nasty bumble bee.
He just won't behave for me.
He's had two chances,
and you only get

OUCH!!

I've got a squished-up bumble bee.
I think I'll take him home with me.
He's soft and cute as cute can be...

and he can never sting me!

ED EMBERLEY AS DRAWN BY
ADRIAN CARNEY FEB 1991

REBECCA EMBERLEY AS DRAWN BY
MICHAEL EMBERLEY DEC 29 1963

MICHAEL EMBERLEY AS DRAWN BY
REBECCA EMBERLEY DEC 28 1963